Mrs. Bunny and Miss Kitty

A different Easter Story

Marianne
Eichenbaum

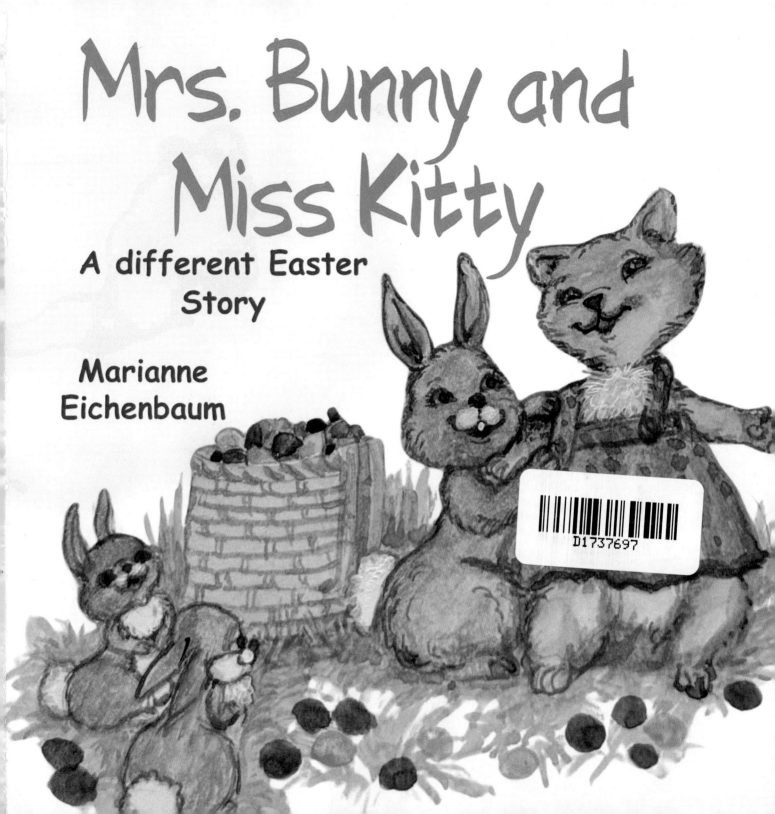

Dedication

This book is dedicated to my talented Artist friend, Susan Graeser who drew and painted the illustrations in this book. Sadly these are her last illustrations before she lost her brave fight against cancer in 2024. I will always miss her!

Marianne

For many springs, Mrs. Bunny had hopped through the meadows, delivering colorful eggs and sweet treats to the children of the town. But now she felt tired, her fluffy ears drooped, and she knew it was time to find someone who could take over being the Easter Bunny. Easter was approaching fast, and Mrs. Bunny felt a flutter of worry in her heart. She gazed at the calendar, her whiskers twitching with concern. Could she really do it all again? Or was it time to find someone new to take over the beloved role of the Easter Bunny?

In the days before Easter, Mrs. Bunny's home was filled with colorful eggs of all shapes and sizes. Each egg sparkled with love and care, ready to be delivered to eager children. Yet, despite the beauty of the eggs around her, Mrs. Bunny couldn't shake the feeling that her days of hopping through town were drawing to a close. "Perhaps this is the last time," she thought, holding a glittering egg in her paw. But who could carry on this special tradition?

One sunny morning, Mrs. Bunny sought advice from her dear friend, Happy Frog, who lounged contentedly on his lily pad. "Happy Frog," she began, her voice soft with concern, "I'm growing too weary to deliver Easter joy to the children. Do you know who could take my place?" Happy Frog's eyes twinkled as he pondered the question. With a hop and a smile, he exclaimed, "Mrs. Bunny, have you considered Miss Kitty? She's graceful and kind, just like you."

Mrs. Bunny's ears perked up. "Miss Kitty? You may be onto something, Happy Frog!" she exclaimed before setting off to find her friend. It didn't take long before she found Miss Kitty basking in the sun, her fur gleaming under the morning light. "Miss Kitty, I need your help," Mrs. Bunny began, explaining her situation. Miss Kitty's emerald eyes widened in surprise. "But I'm just a cat! How could I possibly take your place as the Easter Bunny?"

Mrs. Bunny smiled warmly. "Don't worry, Miss Kitty, I'll teach you everything I know. Together, we can make magic happen!" And so began Miss Kitty's training. Mrs. Bunny showed her how to hop through the fields, gracefully hopping over the tall grass. Miss Kitty was wobbly at first, her paws slipping on the dewy ground. But soon, under Mrs. Bunny's patient guidance, Miss Kitty found a way to hop joyfully through the meadows, her heart light with excitement.

To fully transform into an Easter Bunny, Miss Kitty needed more than just a hop. Mrs. Bunny carefully made a pair of bunny ears for her from large green leaves. As she placed the ears on Miss Kitty's head, a tiny caterpillar watched from the nearby bushes, its eyes wide with curiosity. Miss Kitty glanced at her reflection in the stream and giggled. "I still look like a kitty with big ears!" she laughed, but Mrs. Bunny just smiled. "Trust me, the children will love you."

As Easter morning dawned, the time had come for Miss Kitty to take on her new role. With her bunny ears proudly perched on her head, she filled a large basket with colorful Easter eggs, each one more beautiful than the last. Mrs. Bunny stood beside her smiling, giving a nod of approval. Together, they looked at the basket, filled to the brim with treats for the children, and set off to spread Easter joy.

Miss Kitty hopped through the streets and gardens, her basket swaying gently on her back. Children peeked out from behind curtains, their eyes wide with wonder. "Look! It's the Easter Bunny!" they whispered, delighted by the sight of Miss Kitty in her bunny ears. Some even waved excitedly from their windows. With each house she visited, Miss Kitty left behind bright eggs and candies, her heart swelling with pride as she saw the joy on the children's faces.

By midday, the sun hung high in the sky, casting a golden glow over the town. Miss Kitty had delivered all the Easter eggs, and she returned to Mrs. Bunny's side, her basket now empty but her heart full of happiness. Together, they sat on a grassy hill, looking out over the town below, basking in the warmth of the sun. "You did it, Miss Kitty," Mrs. Bunny said with a smile. "You've brought so much joy to the children today."

As the day drew to a close, Mrs. Bunny and Miss Kitty sat together, watching the sun dip below the horizon. The sky was painted inpretty colors of orange and pink, a perfect ending to a magical day. "Thank you for trusting me, Mrs. Bunny," Miss Kitty said softly. Mrs. Bunny placed her paw on Miss Kitty's. "You've proven that even a cat can be an Easter Bunny," she said warmly. Together, they watched the last light of the day fade, knowing that their friendship would last forever, and many more Easter adventures lay ahead.

The End